Living Solo

A Practical Guide To Life On Your Own

NANCY GOLDNER, PhD LICSW CGP

www.living-solo.com

Living Solo: A Practical Guide To Life On Your Own

Published by the Author

"I Want To Write" from Evidence by Mary Oliver
Published by Beacon Press Boston
Copyright © 2009 by Mary Oliver
Reprinted by Permission of the
Charlotte Sheedy Literary Agency Inc.

Cover and Book Design by Frank Criscione

1st Printing, 2013 ~ Red Sun Press, Boston, MA

ISBN 978-0-615-89080-7

CONTENTS

CONTENTS

I Want To Write Something So Simply

I want to write something
so simply
about love
or about pain
that even
as you are reading
you feel it
and as you read
you keep feeling it
and though it be my story
it will be common,
though it be singular
it will be known to you
so that by the end
you will think –
no, you will realize –
that it was all the while
yourself arranging the words,
that it was all the time
words that you yourself,
out of your own heart
had been saying.

Mary Oliver

INTRODUCTION

Many years ago I wrote a poem that contained the lines, "I am not alone but the culture keeps saying I am." I noted then that when the letter "I" is taken away from the word alone, what is left are the words "a one." Being "a one" conveyed that I did not want to see myself as somehow incomplete that the reference to being a woman alone implied. Instead, I wanted to see myself as a person sufficient in herself although I was without a partner. At that time in the 1970's, as the women's movement asserted, women were still being defined by a dependent relationship with a man. Book titles like "Why Do I Feel Like I Am Nothing Without A Man," "The Cinderella Complex," and "Women Who Love Too Much" found wide circulation. In reaction to this limiting definition, in the years that followed, the women's movement asserted a woman's innate existence as a separate and complete being. That is what inspired my poem.

At that same time, there was no corresponding reference to men without a partner being seen as somehow incomplete. Instead, the popular literature focused much more on the male fear of being in a committed relationship and suppression of their emotions, Hence, book titles like "The Peter Pan Syndrome" and "Why Men are the Way They Are" populated bookstore shelves and even found their way onto the best seller lists. So the incomplete woman and the emotionally stifled and frightened man were the dominant stereotypes about men and women in relationship in those years.

So much has changed since then. Women have come to be seen and to see ourselves as fully autonomous beings while men can now express their longing for intimacy and capacity for nurturance. As these cultural shifts in gender stereotypes have taken place, what has not changed is the human need for connection. Now, the popular press is full of books aimed at giving people the tools for enhancing their partner relationships, relationships that today have become much more egalitarian and gender neutral.

What has also changed is a phenomenal increase in the numbers of us living by ourselves, Compared to the literature on partner relations, I found few books addressed to single people. One of them by Florence Falk published in 2007 is entitled, "On My Own, The Art of Being A Woman Alone." In her book. Falk seems to perpetuate the cultural stereotype of single women as insufficient beings. For example, in the blurb, she writes: "At some point over the course of an American woman's life, she will find herself alone…and when that happens she will be at a loss as to how to handle it." Her perspective is especially evident in the stories she relates of relationship breakups. In these stories, Falk stresses how women need to repair their incapacity for solitude and their sense of incompleteness in order to manage being single.

In another book, "Singled Out: How Singles Are Stereotyped, Stigmatized, and Ignored and Still Live Happily Ever After" published in 2006, Bella Depaulo, the author, dispels 10 myths about singlehood and single life. This book breaks ground by rebutting cultural stereotypes that define single people as inadequate, chronically lonely, unhappy or tragic beings. The author reframes singlehood in a positive way and single life as a viable life style when compared to married life. However, even this author presents married life as the cultural norm with being single a deviant status that needs to be defended.

Currently, the popular press is making much more frequent reference to both the striking demographics of being single and to the single life experience. As a result, I suspect more and more books on this theme will be published. This shift in demographics and the changing view of being single is nicely captured in the headline of a recent news story that appeared in the Boston Globe : "The New Normal: Living Alone." The article noted that 31 million people live alone and that "one-person households make up 28 percent of the total, tying with childless couples as the most common residential type."(1) The article was based on Erik Klinenberg's book, Going Solo: The Extraordinary Rise and Surprising Appeal of Living Alone" published in 2012. Even more striking are the numbers Klinenberg cites - only one person resides in 40 percent or more of all households in Atlanta. Denver, Seattle, San Francisco and Minneapolis while in New York and Washington D.C. the proportion rises to 50 percent. (2)

Yet, the stereotype persists. I hear the words "alone" and "lonely" repeatedly as I listen to a radio talk show with a relationship advice columnist. During the call-in time, I get a chance to point out that the embedded message given to listeners is that being single is a deprived state compared to being with a partner. She responds by saying that being in a troubled marriage can be very lonely so, by comparison, being single will feel better. I fully agree. Nevertheless, with this response, I hear another embedded message - a person with a partner who is not lonely is somehow better off than a single person so why choose to be single.

Perhaps my point of view is skewed by many years of clinical practice with single people and personally being on my own. We are not choosing to be single but single we are. I call this unexpected outcome being circumstantially single rather than single by choice. Living Solo: A Practical Guide to Life on Your Own starts out from the premise that even if it is not turning out as you expected, life on your own can be satisfying and fulfilling. In the chapters that follow, you will hear about the life experiences of many single people including myself, people whom I personally interviewed and, with their permission and identities disguised, some of my therapy clients. I quote from personal interviews in the first person and from clinical material in the third person. My approach is to provide you with an understanding of the emotional impact being single can have and with specific tools for enhancing life on your own.

CHAPTER 1 ~ SOLO IN CONNECTION

We must love or we grow ill.
  ~ Sigmund Freud

The antidote to much anguish is sheer connectedness.
  ~ Irving Yalom

By calling this chapter "Solo in Connection" I emphasize the importance of taking part in an interpersonal world with other people as you go about life on your own. All of us start out in that interpersonal world just by being human. As Sigmund Freud, one of the greatest thinkers about human relationships observed, we are born related. That is, from the moment of our birth we are always oriented toward connecting with others. Freud's term for human emotional bonding is "cathecting," meaning directing our psychic energy toward another person. We "cathect" or channel our psychic energy towards others from the moment of our birth thereby forming emotional bonds or becoming attached. Through our attachments to others throughout our lives, we develop our innate human capacity for emotional intimacy and sociability.

Attachment theorists such as John Bowlby and Mary Ainsworth corroborated and expanded Freud's thinking. They studied infants interacting with their mothers and young children exposed to separation from their parents or parental loss. They discovered that we seek closeness and actively strive to form emotional bonds from a very young age. This ensures our physical survival as infants.

Depending on the quality of the care we receive, the early attachments we form with our caretakers also allow us to feel secure and safe. In their research, Bowlby and Ainsworth found that children sought out mothers who showed a capacity to soothe and comfort them but did not seek out mothers who were distant and rejecting, inconsistently available, intrusive, or frightening On the basis of these differences, the attachments children form are characterized as secure or insecure. (1)

From the different ways our parents interacted with us as infants and young children, we develop distinct patterns of attachment that carry into our adult lives. In other words, the different ways our caretakers responded to us when we sought connection as young children set the stage for how and whether we seek closeness with others in adulthood.

Not surprisingly, secure infants have a much greater chance of forming the kind of emotional bonds in adulthood that provide feelings of safety and security. On the other hand, insecurely attached infants have a much harder time seeking and finding safety and security in adult relationships

Our adult attachment patterns are made up of thoughts and feelings that come up whenever we interact with other people as we go through our daily lives. They include

> ~ the different ways we typically respond on
> a feeling level to other people, for example,
> with suspiciousness or a sense of trust,

~ what ideas we have about ourselves and others,
for example, seeing ourselves and others
as deficient or worthy, and

~ what we usually expect to happen in
relationships, for example, we will be cared
for or abandoned.

Think of these stable ways of thinking and reacting like long-standing habits that shape and organize the ongoing flow of our interaction with others without our being consciously aware of them.

FOUR ADULT ATTACHMENT PATTERNS

In the course of many years of clinical practice with single adults, I came to identify four distinct adult attachment patterns that can get in the way of being a "solo in connection." These four patterns are: the Latchkey Child, the Caretaker Child, the Unloved Child and the Suffocated Child. I base this typology on the framework and findings of the attachment theorists. As the attachment theorists found, our adult attachment patterns develop from childhood experiences with our earliest caretakers. I trace these four attachment patterns back to family history as well as show you how they carry forward into single adulthood in the present.

Of course as discrete types, they are abstractions and you may recognize a little bit of yourself in all of them. I have distilled them from many childhood and adult experiences where the distinctions among them are not so clear cut. Even so, these four types capture the distinct and different ways of thinking, behaving and holding expectations of others that may block single adults from having more satisfying emotional lives.

The Latchkey Child

Picture a child standing before the doorway to a house or an apartment on a school day after the school day ends. She reaches for a key that is hanging from a piece of ribbon around her neck. She opens the door and enters an empty house or apartment. She locks the door behind her and remains there by herself until her parent(s) comes home. She is a "latchkey child."

How might she be feeling? Put yourself in her shoes. Is she a little bit frightened of being on her own? Is she excited by the chance just to "do her own thing" without an adult keeping an eye on her? Is she feeling "at loose ends" not knowing what do with herself? Is she longing to have someone there and not be by herself?

By definition, a latchkey child is a school aged child who after school lets out, regularly lets himself or herself into a house or apartment and for whom there is no adult or older teenager present. (2) In other words, the home life of a certain group of children, usually between the ages of six and twelve but also into the early teenage years, is marked by parental absence for hours at a time during the school year. Where is the adult that is supposed to be there to assure the safety of these children, to provide structure and direction during the after school hours, or just to give them some individual attention after they have been in a classroom full of others until school lets out.

The term "latchkey child" arose during the war years, 1941–45, when women entered the labor force in great numbers. Although there was extensive government support for organized child care arrangements during those years, we can only speculate why some school age children let themselves into an empty house or apartment while their mothers were at work. After government subsidized childcare programs were dismantled in the post-war period, working parents may have had no alternative except to give a child a key because of the continuing gap between the end of the school day and their workday. Even today, when afterschool programs are available to many parents, the US Census found that millions of children still go home to empty houses or apartments where no adult or older teenager is present.

Research on the effects of parental absence on latchkey children finds that children younger than ten report feeling lonely, bored and scared at higher rates compared to children for whom there was adult supervision after school. On the other hand, developmental psychologists see a benefit to children being on their own after school. The enforced solitude of latchkey children offers opportunities for strengthening a sense of autonomy and becoming self reliant at a young age. (3)

ARE YOU A LATCHKEY CHILD?

FROM AN EARLY AGE, WERE YOU ON YOUR OWN AFTER SCHOOL IN AN EMPTY HOUSE OR APARTMENT?

DID YOU WEAR A HOUSE KEY ON A STRING AROUND YOUR NECK OR GET IT FROM A HIDING PLACE NEAR YOUR FRONT DOOR?

DID YOUR PARENTS ADMONISH YOU NOT TO LEAVE THE HOUSE OR APARTMENT ONCE YOU CAME HOME FROM SCHOOL AND TO KEEP THE DOOR LOCKED?

IN YOUR LIFE IN THE HERE AND NOW, DO YOU FEEL QUITE SELF SUFFICIENT – A STRONG SENSE OF BEING ABLE TO TAKE CARE OF YOURSELF, NOT RELYING ON HELP FROM OTHERS?

IS IT HARD TO ASK OTHERS FOR HELP?
DO YOU FEEL UNCOMFORTABLE BEING BY YOURSELF AND TEND TO SURROUND YOURSELF WITH PEOPLE?

Patty, A Latchkey Child

Patty, a widowed woman in her 50's, describes herself as an extremely independent and self reliant person. She attributes this to her childhood years during which her working mother was often out of the house while she and her sister were often left to fend for themselves. Her mother's absences from home continued long after her parents divorced when Patty was six years old. Patty adapted to her "latchkey" childhood by having a very active social life and extensive social network. In this way, by making certain she would be with other children after school hours, she avoided the typical loneliness latchkey children feel. By having a large group of friends and active social life, Patty continued this adaptation well into her adult life although after marrying and becoming a parent, she focused much more on family life.

Patty weathered the death of her partner some years ago with the ongoing support of her many friends and religious community. She made up for the loss of her family life by surrounding herself with other people, often organizing communal meals. However, as the years passed, she inevitably ended up spending more time by herself. This would happen when her children were occupied elsewhere and her mostly married friends were unavailable to socialize with her. At these times, Patty became acutely aware how uncomfortable she is and how lonely she feels just being by herself. She realized that her sociability enabled her to avoid this discomfort. She also came to understand this reaction as the legacy of her "latchkey" childhood. From this awareness, she began to develop a sense of being enough in herself, that is, she became much more comfortable with spending time by herself and even began to enjoy her solitude.

The Caretaker Child

Caretakers are made, not born. I think this as I consider this particular adult attachment pattern and its origins in childhood. Understanding how they are made comes from Salvadore Minuchin, a leading family therapist and his colleagues who coined the term "parentified child" in 1967. By "parentified, " Minuchin and his colleagues meant that instead of being cared for by our parents, we take on the parental role and become their caretakers, and, in many instances, the caretakers for our siblings as well. Parenting our parent and our siblings involves meeting their emotional needs for nurturance, protection and attention. It can also involve the physical care of the home and family members. It goes without saying the parentified child's emotional and physical needs are unmet.

Typically, a parentified child comes from a family where for a variety of reasons the adults are unable to function adequately in the parental role. This could be because they are substance abusers, mentally ill, physically disabled, victims or perpetrators of domestic violence, or have personality deficits that arose out of their own unmet childhood needs. Whatever the reason, passing the caretaking responsibility to a child robs that child of childhood.

By the time parentified children reach adulthood, the pattern of meeting other people's emotional needs has been well established. Grown up parentified children easily find people to take care of. Caretaking others is a dependable way to have a connection with people but it comes at a very high cost to our own emotional and physical well being.

ARE YOU A CARETAKER?

AS A CHILD, DID YOU TEND TO YOUR PARENT'S FEELINGS AND NEEDS WHILE YOURS WERE NOT SEEN OR HEARD?

WERE YOU PUT IN CHARGE OF YOUNGER SIBLINGS?

DO YOU FIND YOURSELF IN RELATIONSHIPS WITH "TAKERS," FRIENDS AND FAMILY MEMBERS WHO EXPECT YOU TO MEET THEIR NEEDS AND TEND TO THEIR FEELINGS WITHOUT GIVING TIME AND ATTENTION IN RETURN?

DO YOU FIND IT HARD TO ASK OTHER PEOPLE FOR THEIR TIME AND ATTENTION ?

DO YOU OVERWORK, SPEND MANY MORE HOURS AT WORK THAN YOU ARE BEING PAID FOR ?

DO YOU OFTEN FEEL DEPLETED, EXHAUSTED, "SUCKED DRY" BY ALL THE DEMANDS PEOPLE IN YOUR LIFE PLACE ON YOU?

DO YOU FIND IT DIFFICULT TO SET ASIDE TIME FOR FUN OR THINGS THAT GIVE YOU PLEASURE OUTSIDE OF WORKING HOURS?

DO YOU DESPAIR OF FEELING CARED FOR BY ANY OF THE PEOPLE IN YOUR LIFE?

Jack A Caretaker Child

Jack is a 43 year old single man who repeatedly finds himself being a caretaker to women in his life. He would be extremely attentive, nurturing and available to these women. However, he hardly ever received their interest and concern in return. So, while being the caretaker enabled him to be in relationships, what he gave he rarely got back. Ultimately, these relationships would prove unsatisfying, especially because Jack would experience a lack of a deep emotional connection. Jack would then end them with a sigh of relief not to be burdened any longer by meeting their needs while his got neglected.

In seeking insight into his attachment pattern, Jack came to understand its roots in the relationship he had with his highly self absorbed mother and younger sister. Jack's parents separated when he was quite young. From then on, Jack became the caretaker for his younger sister as she turned to him for the emotional nurturance their mother was unable to give. At the same time, his mother demanded his attention, wanting his admiration and declarations of love for her, something that has persisted into their relationship in the present.

As Jack became increasingly aware of being caught in the caretaking role in his relationships with women, he became determined to stop repeating this pattern. A turning point came for Jack when he underwent surgery. He needed another person to accompany him home from the hospital and to look after him when he was home convalescing. For the first time in his life, Jack allowed himself "to lean," that is, to reach out to another person for caretaking (in this instance, a long term friend from whom he'd never previously asked for help). Jack not only behaved differently but, as a result, new feelings came up for Jack, especially a feeling of closeness to his friend and of being nurtured and protected by another person.

The Unloved Child

It is said that the first love in a woman's life is her father. The same goes for men – his mother being a man's first love. Perhaps this was not true for you and you grew up a fatherless daughter or a motherless son. But even if your father or mother was not physically present, he or she may have existed for you in fantasy. So, whether real or imagined, fathers and mothers loom large as women and men pass from childhood through adolescence to adult womanhood and manhood.

Starting in the 1990's, an emerging body of research findings affirms the significant impact a father has on his daughter's emotional development. Researchers found that when fathers are appropriately loving and present, daughters grow up with a strong sense of self worth, are comfortable with being a woman and do not fear intimacy. On the other hand, fathers who are aloof, intimidating, abusive, or present only intermittently with limited contact seriously affect a girl's self esteem. Daughters take a father's rejection personally and grow up feeling unworthy and unlovable. This makes it very difficult to become emotionally close, to trust loving feelings when these are expressed and to be self protective. (4)

What about unloved sons? How does an unloving mother affect a man's emotional development? According to Peggy Streep, writing in Psychology Today: "the legacy of an unloving mother spills over into a man's psyche and ability to connect to women in ways that are unique."(5) In childhood, this may manifest as "relational aggression" toward other children while in adulthood, "it is harder for a man to acknowledge the [emotional] pain he is experiencing and the ways in which is affecting his intimate relationships."(6) However, Streep emphasizes that both men and women unloved as children exhibit the "seven common wounds of insecure attachment: a lack of confidence, a lack of trust, trouble setting boundaries, difficulty seeing the self accurately, avoiding connection, overeating, and replicating the [insecure] bond in other relationships. (7)

ARE YOU AN UNLOVED CHILD?

WHEN YOU DEVELOP FEELINGS FOR A NEW PERSON IN YOUR LIFE, DO YOU START TO WORRY RIGHT AWAY THAT THE PERSON WILL REJECT YOU?

DO YOU BELIEVE THERE MUST BE "SOMETHING WRONG WITH ME" BECAUSE YOU ARE "STILL" SINGLE AND OTHERS MUST THINK SO, TOO?
DO YOU FEAR YOU WILL NEVER HAVE PARTNER?

AS A YOUNG GIRL OR BOY, DID YOU RECEIVE AN AP-
PROPRIATE ACKNOWLEDGEMENT AND APPRECIA-
TION OF YOUR BUDDING SEXUAL MATURITY FROM
YOUR OPPOSITE SEX PARENT OR WERE YOU MADE
TO FEEL UNCOMFORTABLE?

WAS LITTLE INTEREST SHOWN IN YOU AND WERE
YOU MOSTLY IGNORED BY YOUR OPPOSITE SEX PAR-
ENT?

WAS THERE A SENSE OF EMOTIONAL DISTANCE BE-
TWEEN YOU AND YOUR OPPOSITE SEX PARENT?

WERE YOU NEGLECTED OR ABANDONED BY YOUR
OPPOSITE SEX PARENT AFTER YOUR PARENTS DI-
VORCED?

WERE YOU PUT DOWN, DEMEANED, INSULTED, OB-
JECTIFIED, OR ABUSED BY YOUR OPPOSITE SEX PAR-
ENT?

Carla, An Unloved Daughter

Carla is a very attractive, divorced woman in her
mid forties who feels hopeless about ever finding
a new partner. She sees herself as unattractive,
having compared herself all her life to her sister
who she sees as much prettier than she is. As a
teenager, she hardly dated. The man she eventually married is one of the few she dated as a
young woman.

There is a strong sense of her father's absence from early in Carla's life. When speaking about their relationship, Carla is dismissive of there being any emotional connection between them. She does not recall ever receiving praise from him or having him show any interest in her. She describes him as distant and uncommunicative as if he rarely noticed her at all. After her parents divorced, there was even less father-daughter contact.

When the connection was made between Carla's sense of hopelessness and unlovability in relation to men and the lack of emotional nurturance from her father, she could begin to think differently about herself. She could start to build a much more positive sense of herself as lovable and desirable. She no longer had to believe there was something wrong with her for "still being single."

The Suffocated Child

"Overparented and Underhappy" - so says the headline of a newspaper article about the effect "helicopter parents" have on their children's well being. The article reports on research conducted with college students whose parents were overprotective and overinvolved in their lives. The image of a helicopter hovering over the same spot has come to be used to describe this kind of parent.

Another study had similar findings. In this study, students with helicopter parents showed less openness to new ideas and actions and higher usage of prescription medications for anxiety and depression compared with students whose parents kept more of a distance. This study also found that most of the "hovering" was being done by mothers. (8)

I have not found any research on what adult children of "helicopter parents" experience in adulthood. But, a very similar back story emerges for single adults I have seen in my clinical practice. These are both men and women and they range in age from their thirties to their seventies. A common thread running through their childhood and well into adulthood is the presence of an intrusive, anxious parent who demands frequent contact. This inhibits them from being comfortable with emotional closeness as it begins to feel oppressive and trigger a fear of losing a sense of being a separate person in his or her own right.

A child of a "helicopter parent" was never given "room to breathe" which makes it difficult to grow into being a separate self, capable of making autonomous decisions in his or her own best interest. It also thwarts being open to freely explore and experiment – to learn new things or go new places The parental message to grown up suffocated children may still convey discouragement of trying something new such as a new profession or a geographic move.

The fear of having "no room to breathe" also understandably surfaces as emotional closeness with others takes place in adulthood. This feeling often gets expressed as "needing space." Fortunately, with self awareness and the support of therapy, suffocated children become more comfortable with emotional closeness, firmer in their boundaries in interaction with an intrusive parent and much more open to life changing decisions.

ARE YOU A SUFFOCATED CHILD?

WHEN YOU WERE A CHILD, DID YOUR PARENT HOVER NERVOUSLY AROUND YOU, KEEPING VERY CLOSE TABS ON ALL YOUR COMINGS AND GOINGS? DID YOUR PARENTS' FEAR TAKING RISKS? DOES THIS KEEP YOU FROM TRYING OUT NEW THINGS?

DO YOU FIND IT DIFFICULT TO DECIDE WHAT YOU WANT TO DO, TO MAKE PLANS AND FOLLOW THROUGH WITH THEM OR TO CARVE OUT A PATH FOR YOURSELF IN TERMS OF YOUR WORK LIFE AND LIFE OUTSIDE OF WORK?

WHEN YOU START TO GET EMOTIONALLY CLOSE TO SOMEONE NEW IN YOUR LIFE, DO YOU FEAR YOU WILL LOSE BEING IN CHARGE OF YOUR OWN TIME?

DO YOU EXPERIENCE A DESIRE FOR EMOTIONAL CLOSENESS WITH YOU AS AN UNREASONABLE DE-MAND ON YOUR TIME OR FEELINGS?

ARE YOU MOST COMFORTABLE WHEN YOU ARE BY YOURSELF?

John, A Suffocated Child

John, a social worker in his thirties, has a deep longing to be involved with a woman but a need for emotional distance soon surfaces when he becomes involved in a new relationship. Eventually, he backs off. John grew up with the typical "helicopter parent," in this instance, a mother who kept close tabs on him and also demanded a lot of his attention. This was only intensified by his mother's life threatening illness when John was in high school.

After John moved out on his own in his twenties, his mother continued to demand attention. This took the form of inviting herself to spend time with him or insisting that he return home to spend time with her. John often chose not to respond to his mother's frequent communications just to keep his peace of mind but nevertheless often felt stirred to anger whenever his mother's emails, texts or phone messages would appear.

Through therapy, John learned to set limits of his mother's demands and not allow himself to be triggered into anger. He also became aware how being a suffocated child inhibited him from emotional intimacy with a partner. This new awareness gave him the courage to risk emotional closeness without fear of losing himself.

OBSERVE, REFLECT AND PRACTICE

Patty, Jack, Carla and John point the way toward how patterns can shift and new ways of thinking and behaving become established. By observing their reactions in relationships with people in their lives, their thoughts about themselves, and how they regard others, they became aware of their adult attachment patterns. By reflecting on these patterns, they came to understand their origins in the past and also began to experiment with thinking and behaving differently.

Perhaps you may now be wondering, how you recognize and unlearn your old ways? Your old ways of thinking and behaving feel so familiar, so much part of who you are and how you see yourself and others. Yet, you do know that you are not having the life you want. Too often, you feel sad, hurt, deprived, angry, lonely, frustrated, neglected, hopeless or worried. Not only would you like these feelings to happen much less frequently but, my personal and clinical experience tells me, you want to feel more content with the life you are making for yourself.

Clearly, just as Patty, Jack, Carla and John found, one answer lies in learning new ways of thinking and behaving. Fortunately, to accomplish this, you can draw upon your capacity to observe and reflect. It is this capacity that brings us to self awareness and begins the learning process. As Carla, Jack, Patty and John show us, our old ways of thinking and behaving become alien to us. We begin to catch ourselves enacting them. But this learning does not take place without practice. In other words, with self awareness we can start to experiment with acting and thinking differently as Carla, Jack, Patty and John have done. With experimentation, new interpersonal experiences take place that trigger new feelings, thoughts and attitudes.

The interpersonal neurobiologists weigh in here in a very striking way. They correlate stable patterns of attachment formed in childhood with deeply embedded, extremely complex neural networks that get activated in our relationships with other people throughout our lives. Although it is not in our conscious awareness, when this occurs in interaction with others, measurable physiological changes take place in our bodies such as the release of cortisol, the stress hormone, or the release of oxytocin and the endorphins, the brain chemicals associated with feelings of well-being In other words, as you express feelings, think about and behave towards other people in the ongoing stream of your everyday life, you are activating a "social synapse." The "social synapse" specifically refers to the powerful biochemical changes that take place when we interact with others. The interpersonal neurobiologists refer to this biochemical process as the functioning of the "social brain."

The interpersonal neurobiologists also tell us that, as adults, we can map new neural networks. They refer to this remapping capacity of the brain as its "neuroplasticity." The remapping process is triggered, first and foremost, by our becoming consciously aware of our attachment patterns, that is, by observing how we typically respond emotionally to other people, what persistent ideas we carry about ourselves and other people, and our usual expectations of how others will think about and behave towards us. Once we become aware of our patterns, we can use our awareness to shape new ways of thinking and behaving. When we do this, we remap our "social brain." When our adult attachment patterns shift, the "social synapse" itself activates different neural pathways and, correspondingly, new biochemical processes. This is especially significant for our emotional health. A decrease in the level of cortisol, the stress hormone, released into our bloodstreams means we feel calmer and less anxious in interaction with others while with the release of oxytocin and the endorphins, we feel safer and more relaxed. As we practice new ways of behaving, have new thoughts and experience new feelings, we are remapping the neural pathways that make up our "social brain" and modifying the biochemical processes that make up the "social synapse."

BEGIN WITH SELF AWARENESS

Awareness is learning to keep yourself company.
  ~ Geneen Roth

The "how-to" of shifting old patterns begins with you becoming self aware. Observing yourself may not be something you are familiar with and you may be wondering how to go about it. Think of yourself taking a picture of you as if your conscious awareness is like a video camera that records your inner thoughts and feeling states, not just images. Turn on the camera and start noticing your response in a particular moment of contact with someone in your personal life. Where are you? Are you at home? At work? Coming in the door? Out and about? By yourself? If with another or others, with whom? What feelings are you having? Are you angry? Hurt? Deprived? Sad? Lonely? Frustrated? Hopeless? Worried? Disappointed? When else have you felt that way? What memories come up for you?

Writing down what you observe may help you develop your capacity to be self aware. However, if you tend to be self critical when you look inward, you are no longer a "camera" but you have become a judge. Sitting in harsh judgment on yourself is not the kind of self observation I am directing you towards. Rather, this method of self exploration absolutely requires being compassionate towards yourself.

Here from my own life are two examples of observing, reflecting and practicing that brought me to new feelings, thoughts and behaviors.

A Latchkey Child Observes, Reflects and Practices

Whenever I go out, I find myself checking whether I have my house keys even though I also know I just put them in their usual place in my purse. I wonder why I keep doing this and I begin to question my habitual key checking behavior. As I consider it, a painful memory is evoked.

I remember as a seventh grader in elementary school coming home for lunch to an empty house. I remember going to the side door of my house and opening the door, using my house key that I carry in a little pouch labeled "back door key." I come up a few steps into the kitchen. A sandwich my mother has prepared is sitting on the kitchen table. The kitchen is very quiet with just me there. The memory is painful as I look back. I put myself in the moment to see if I can recall the feelings I was having. As I recall how I felt in that situation, it seems I was quite detached. In other words, I suppressed the sadness and worry I was feeling at having to come home, sit and have lunch, and return to school all by myself but in remembering it in the present, these are the feelings that come up. It scared me.

As I make this connection, I remind myself that while a "latchkey child" is bereft of an adult presence, an adult living solo can learn to be sufficiently present to herself. Affirming that my keys are in their usual place as I leave my apartment restores a feeling of safety rather than feeling abandoned and scared. Now that I have made this connection, when I leave my apartment. I can just go on my way without stopping to check if the keys are with me. I feel comforted by having this choice and also somehow freer by my coming to understand the old pattern and being able to act differently.

An Unloved Daughter Observes, Reflects and Practices

As I am out and about, I notice that I have a heightened awareness of fathers interacting with daughters -- a father and a teenage daughter talking in an animated way as they walk together, a father holding the hand of a young daughter as they cross the street, a father leaning down to plant a kiss on a infant daughter's cheek. Strong feelings come up for me when I observe fathers and daughters interacting in loving ways. I feel a deep sadness and a keen sense of deprivation as I notice this. I have had this reaction all my adult life and I wonder if I will always have it. I do not have any memories like this in relation to my father. I recall him as an absence in my younger years as he absorbed himself with his work and outside interests and as a dangerous and intrusive figure in my teenage years of budding sexuality.

As I reflect on my reaction and make the connection to my relationship with my father, I think a powerful new thought: "that's about him, not me." In other words, my father was incapable of being the loving father I needed him to be. In saying this, I affirm that in the here and now of my life, whatever message I internalized in the past, I can think of myself as a lovable and desirable woman. I also affirm that as an adult woman, I can appreciate and trust men who behave lovingly to their daughters and show interest in them while maintaining appropriate boundaries, even though as a child and young girl I had little experience of a father like that. By thinking this new way about myself and men as fathers, I establish a new emotional pathway for myself. .As I become aware of the source of my feelings in the past and have new thoughts and feelings in the present, my sadness leaves.

WHAT ABOUT THERAPY?

In my experience, when single people enter therapy, we are often motivated by wanting to know what stands in the way of forming satisfying emotional bonds with a "significant other." However, even coming to an understanding of what stands in our way, emotional intimacy with a "significant other" may not come about. I think of this as being circumstantially single and it is a life situation millions of us are in (see Introduction).

As Carla, Jack, Patty and John show us, resolving what gets in their way of being close to others and seeing yourself in a more favorable light gives you a chance to have a more satisfying interpersonal life living solo. The satisfaction may come from new feelings of being loved, cared for, nurtured, and appreciated, new ideas about yourself and others and new ways of behaving. That is why understanding how your old attachment patterns affect you becomes central to achieving a more fulfilling life as a single person

In answering the questions posed for a Caretaker Child, you may have become aware that you are in one-way relationships with friends and co-workers, giving a lot but getting little in return. Likewise, in answering the questions posed for a Latchkey Child, you may have become aware of a tendency to avoid spending time by yourself. In answering the questions posed for an Unloved Child, you may have become aware that you expect people to have little interest in you. And, in answering the questions posed for a Suffocated Child, you may have become aware that you tend to run from emotional closeness. In short, self awareness is essential to beginning the process of shifting old attachment patterns.

As you bring your attention to your usual way of being with others, consider psychotherapy as a useful way to increase and expand self awareness. The time you spend with a therapist can give you a unique chance to get feedback as you observe and reflect on the ways you usually think and behave. It also can help you be alert to being self-critical if that is your tendency and to become more compassionate towards yourself as you look inward. In other words, therapy gives you a chance to observe yourself enacting, reacting, and thinking in the old ways, to get support in learning and practicing new ways to think and feel, and to do this without becoming self-attacking. A therapist's consistent positive regard for you as you look inward also can help to establish and strengthen positive thoughts and feelings about yourself.

Just as useful in this journey of self discovery is taking part in a therapy group. Think of the therapy group as a "human relations laboratory." In the here and now of a group, a Latch Key Child may find it hard to ask for help from the group or to show a deep longing for their support, a Caretaker Child may be very interested in being of help to other group members but may not ask for any time for herself or himself. The Unloved Child may have great difficulty showing warm feelings towards other group members out of fear of rejection or trusting their warm feelings. The Suffocated Child may find it difficult to stay in the group when feeling trapped and emotional demands start to come up. Feedback from your group therapist and the other group members in reaction to all these old ways of thinking and behaving is a powerful force in bringing about shifts in the old patterns. Taking part in a group also gives group members a unique chance to experience new feelings that come from experimenting with new ways of behaving.

WHY BOND SOLO

In her research on mothers, infants and young children, Ainsworth established five criteria for emotional bonds or attachment. These are:

1) Persistence through time

2) A tie with a particular person who is not interchangeable with anyone else

3) An emotionally significant relationship

4) A wish to maintain proximity or contact

5) A feeling of sadness or distress at separation (9)

Ainsworth's criteria can easily apply to your relationships in later life except that, unlike infants and young children, the extent and intensity of your bonds with others may vary considerably. For example, you may have a large network of acquaintances but only a few close the friends with whom you feel a strong tie. You may have "activity pals" with whom you share mutual interests but with whom you are not especially close. You may feel close or be emotionally distant from family members or even be estranged from them. Or, perhaps, none of Ainsworth's criteria apply and you see yourself as a "loner."

As a single adult, your ties with others are not as critical to your survival as they are to an infant or young child. So, why should you be concerned about being connected to others? The compelling answer is that, by forming bonds with others, you enhance your chances of living a longer and healthier life. Health researchers have found that being socially connected protects our emotional and physical wellbeing. Adults who are socially connected show better health on many health indicators such as recovery rates from surgery, adapting to life with a chronic illness, and self reports of health status and mood. On the other hand, adults who are socially isolated with few social ties, who rarely participate in social activities and who frequently experience feelings of loneliness are at higher risk for impaired physical health, depression and even premature death. (10) Your social connections with others - friends, non-toxic family members, co-workers, colleagues, neighbors, neighbors' or friends' children, your own children if you have children, members of whatever groups to which you belong - these are the kinds of ties that can sustain you as you carry on with life on your own.

CHAPTER 2 ~ CLIMBING THE AGE LADDER SOLO

To exist is to change, to change is to mature, to mature is to create oneself endlessly.
~ Henri Bergson

It did not turn out as I expected. I started out in my twenties as a young married woman and now many decades later, I have been single most of my adult life. As the years passed, staying single kept demanding shifts in my expectations of the life I was living. As I climbed the age ladder, if I was to thrive, I needed to find the inner and outer resources to adapt to continuing to be single. My need to adapt did not mean that I did not desire an intimate and long lasting partnership with someone, a "significant other." It just did not happen for me for a variety of reasons.

Over many years of life on my own, I came to learn an invaluable life lesson. It is better to adapt than to be stuck in perpetual mourning for what I may not get to have. In other words, it is better to adapt than to live life from a position of deprivation. I learned to accept the loss of what I might not get to have rather than getting flattened emotionally by disappointment - to "roll with the punches." Most important of all, I learned to live richly and well as a person on my own in the here-and-now.

Of course, it is frustrating not to have what we expected to have, to have our desires and hopes thwarted. But, it is out of this frustration that we can engage our capacity to adapt and tap into the inner and outer resources that lead to greater life satisfaction. In doing so, we embody Freud's maxim that without frustration there is no growth.

The experiences of other single people whom I interviewed or who were my therapy clients echo my own. In the sections that follow, you will hear from single people from age 31 to age 80. You will find that they have a lot to teach about adaptation as a powerful force in human life as they climbed the age ladder and faced making crucial life choices.

THE BIG IF

A 35 year old asks, "Will I be sitting on my couch by myself when I am 50?" A 38 year old asks, "Will I regret not having children when I reach age 50?" A 44 year old asks, "Have I gotten past my 'sell-by' date?" A 46 year old observes, "I was so angry that I didn't get married and have children." A 50 year old reflects, "I thought I'd have one life but I am having a second life...I thought I'd be married, but I don't have a partner and I am alone."

As their words poignantly tell you, in the decades of the thirties and forties, single people face the future with a great deal of uncertainty. What was supposed to happen by this age did not happen. So, naturally they wonder - will it happen at all? Will I find a partner? Will I have a child of my own? These questions come up for single people of both sexes and every sexual orientation. These questions come up even if someone may not be immediately "driven by the desire to be in a relationship or have a child" (a 38 year old speaking).

Single people in the decades of the thirties and forties tell me that reaching age 50 seems to them to mark an end to the possibility of finding a partner or becoming the parent of a child. Despite this belief, this does not have to be the case. These days, single men and women past 50 can have biological children through a variety of means while throughout our lives, there is always the possibility of intimate partnership. Nevertheless, the age 50 marker symbolizes a fear that neither will happen. After all, the relentless "biological clock" is ticking away for both men and women because as sperm and eggs age, the well-known risks of birth defects and infertility increase. If finding a partner or becoming a parent has not happened by the decades of the thirties and forties, especially with age 50 looming, this is a very understandable fear.

An Antidote To The Accumulation of Regret

As we climb the age ladder, uncertainty over whether or not we remain single stays with us. We are not in complete control of this particular fate even if we are open to and hopeful about the possibility of finding a partner. However, there is one part of life over which we can have a much greater degree of control - whether or not to have a child.

Irving Yalom, in "Staring at the Sun: Overcoming the Dread of Death" speaks of an "awakening moment." This the moment when a person facing a life threatening illness awakens to the realization that the time left before his or her life comes to an end is foreshortened. He goes on to say that taking action in response to this awakening moment provides a guarantee to the dying person against an "accumulation of regret." In saying this, Yalom is well aware, we all "accumulate" regrets as we go through life. At this point, however, when the time left is so short, why accumulate more. Whether it is about repairing a relationship or fulfilling a dream, Yalom tells the dying person to be decisive and take action.

I incorporate Yalom's advice in what I call "an antidote to the accumulation of regret," that is, how you respond to your "awakening moment" with regard to the supposed lost possibility of parenthood that being single involves. If you feel an intense longing for a child of your own when you spend time with your friends' children or your nieces and nephews or as an adorable toddler passes by in a stroller, you have a chance to make a crucial life choice. You could become a single parent by choice. Jane Mattes, a single parent, a psychotherapist, and the founder of Single Mothers by Choice puts it this way: "[you can]reverse the cart and the horse. One thing has to be done in a timely manner, the other [finding a partner] you can do anytime." (1)

Ask yourself this deeply personal and fateful existential question, "will you painfully regret not having a child of your own when you reach your late forties or enter the decade of your fifties?" It is not the decision itself whether to pursue single parenthood that is critical for the avoidance of regret. Rather, it is coming to the decision. The phrase "decision by default" will apply to you if you passively sit with your unfulfilled longing for a child of your own and let the years pass.

In Jane Mattes' experience, the risk of "accumulating regret" is high so she advises you to "come to a decision to take the leap [into single parenthood] or decide not to." (2) Since this is such a fateful decision, you may rightfully be concerned whether a "yes" or "no" is a better fit for you and what to consider in deciding. Jane Mattes found herself unexpectedly pregnant 30 years ago and went on to have a child on her own, inspiring her to found Single Mothers by Choice.

Jane counsels you to consider if you "have the courage to go down a non-traditional path." Below, she distills the wisdom gained from her own experience as a single parent and the 30 years her organization has existed.

> It takes a certain person who is comfortable enough to do that. It is certainly easier these days because such a small percentage of families are the traditional (two-parent) family. Some women have gone through the process and think this is the leap. But, really, it's about having a non-traditional family, not having that second parent - that is the leap they may not feel comfortable taking. (3)

Along with courage, Jane Mattes points to a willingness to put your own needs aside and put your child's needs first is absolutely critical in deciding to pursue parenthood on your own. She also points to a readiness to "settle down" into family life albeit without a partner. (4) There are other factors to bring into your decision process including your finances and the level of acceptance and support you can expect from family and friends.

DO YOU HAVE THE COURAGE TO CHALLENGE CONVENTION AND BECOME THE HEAD OF A NON-TRADITIONAL HOUSEHOLD?

ARE YOU WILLING TO PUT YOUR OWN NEEDS ASIDE AND PUT YOUR CHILD'S NEEDS FIRST?

ARE YOU READY TO SETTLE DOWN AND BE FAMILY-ORIENTED IN YOUR EVERYDAY LIFE?

DO YOU HAVE THE FINANCIAL MEANS TO PAY FOR SURROGANCY, REPRODUCTIVE TECHNOLOGY OR ADOPTION? IF NOT, WOULD YOU CONSIDER A FOSTER CHILD?

DOES YOUR FAMILY SUPPORT YOUR DECISION TO PURSUE SINGLE PARENTHOOD?

WILL YOU BE ABLE TO CALL ON FAMILY MEMBERS AND FRIENDS FOR HELP?

If you answered "yes" to all of these questions, you have the inner and outer resources that can support you in "taking the leap" to have a child of your own on your own. These were the questions Amanda, a single woman in her forties had to answer for herself. In excerpts from my interview with her, she tells about the leap she took and what led up to it.

Amanda Decides to Adopt

Some people have a life plan. I've never had a life plan. I've made some choices but never by 30 I want to be married and by this date [to have a child]. I see why people do that now because if you don't have goals it might not happen. [At age 39, Amanda tried donor insemination]. I felt hugely relieved the first time I was doing it because I realized what I was worried about was would I do it. The whole issue of being pregnant I actually had trouble with, no one expects me to be pregnant...I was Okay with the kid part but I wasn't comfortable with the other part. It was helpful to me to get a grip on my feelings coping with the reality, not hold it all in.

By the end of 2009, my cycles were irregular and I was already in peri-menopause and it just wasn't working so I kind of gave up. At that time I had a friend doing the same thing and I ran in to her and we realized we were both in the same boat which was great. I like her and we could relate and talk about stuff. So we went to a Resolve conference where they had all this stuff about infertility but also about choices. I went to a workshop on adoption. I was sitting there and then something struck me: whatever happens if you persevere and you don't give up you will have a child. I was very moved by that. I always wanted a piece of my heritage, my family. That's what I always envisioned. With adoption it's about becoming a parent. So I looked at it in a new way. I started the [adoption] process in the Fall of 2010. It took a little while [after the Resolve conference] because through it all I was still processing "this is not my beautiful life, this is not how it's supposed to be." So I was not feeling totally great about it all the time. But never questioning that I do want to be a parent. I know it's the right thing for me.

[For support] there's the [Singles Mothers By Choice] community and a bunch of single women pursuing adoption through my agency. They sponsor a support group so I hope I can stay in touch with some of them. Two of the women got babies and they came back with their babies and told their stories of what they had gone through and it was really great to see the reality of it actually happening. Here they are with their babies. At the next meeting it could be me. When I think about support I first think about my friends and family. My Mom said she wants to come with me when I go to adopt the kid. (5)

Amanda's experience conveys the thoughtfulness and time that goes into the decision to become a single parent. Amanda's experience also tells you that being resourceful in seeking out information and peer support play a crucial part in the process. After many months of waiting to adopt, Amanda is now the mother of a baby girl.

What about single men who long to have a child? These days, whether through surrogacy, adoption or fostering a child, single men are becoming fathers in ever increasing numbers. As Adam Pertman, Director of the Evan B. Donaldson Adoption Institute told me:

> The trend is everywhere, aided and abetted by gay parents. It becomes a phenomenon that feeds itself as more people see it's possible and see it's all right, [this] grows the pool of prospective parents. The more they see it, the more likely they say, I can do it."(6)

If you are a man on your own reading this and you answered "yes" to the questions I posed earlier, consider following Yalom's dictum not to accumulate regret. Take the leap Jane Mattes speaks of. Decide to fulfill your longing to have a child and become a parent. Once you've taken the leap, then you can pursue the array of available resources in support of your decision.

What Adult Children of Single Parents By Choice Say

Having come to the decision to pursue having a child on your own, there are two pressing questions you may be asking yourself: "What about my child's feelings about my decision? How will I respond to them?" I did not include these two questions in my earlier list because they follow upon your decisive "yes" to the questions posed on that list. But understandably, they are of concern.

In New York City on October 15, 2011, 300 people from 19 states and six countries gathered to commemorate the 30th anniversary of the founding of Single Mothers By Choice. Three adult children of mothers who chose single parenthood, Hannah, Eric and Laura Beth, took part in a panel discussion on the theme "What I Wish My Mom had Known, What Was It like, What I Wish I had Known.". This gives you a unique chance to hear from them directly.

Laura Beth, An Adopted Daughter

The most important thing about growing up is that attitude is everything. What I've observed from looking at my Mom and her friends who are also single mothers, you're defined by something you lack if you lack a partner, if you are a single Mom. [Instead] I was taught that my family was complete. It was me, my Mom, a dog and a cat. That was about it...I grew up thinking this was normal. It's so much part of who I am that it's hard to answer the question when people ask: what is it like or would you want a Dad. I joke with her that we should celebrate Father's Day, get you a cigar. My Mom to me has been both parents.

I heard someone earlier feeling angry that your parent had chosen to do it by herself. I think again that's two sides of the coin. It's a wonderful thing that she did what she wanted to do on her own but I think you have to understand that the decisions you make shape your child's world. My Mom was very good in building in places where I could ask those questions...Overall, there's a lot I wish I had known or my Mom had known but I think that ultimately that's what life's about, the things you don't know that strengthen you and get you to ask the right questions and get your children to ask the right questions.

Eric, Son of the Founder of Single Mothers By Choice

I grew up surrounded. I had the confidence that this is something that people do. It's important to have a network of people doing what you do so your child can see that. It was unusual and I know that. When I was younger I didn't talk about it. I wish I had known how to talk about it.

Your demonstrated attitudes towards the concept will be passed onto your child so you have to handle the situation with the attitude, this is fine, A Dad is not part of your family and as a child you can say that with conviction, but if it's not clear, then it's hard to say with conviction.

I wish I'd had more of an understanding of the importance of male role models when I was very young. She did a big favor to me by making sure I had older men in my life whom she trusted and I trusted. And she encouraged me to play sports which put me in front of coaches and other guys my age. I didn't quite get it at the time when she signed me up for the Big Brother program. The Big Brother who was assigned to me became a very good friend of mine. I would encourage all of you to do that as well.

Hannah, A Donor Daughter

It's a non-issue for me, the way I grew up. That's what I knew, that's what seemed normal, my family. I was aware when I went to school people had their Dads dropping them off.

Through the years it's been much the same. It hasn't been an issue or kept me from being friends with someone, from forming relationships. When it did come up people were sort of indifferent. It's easier now that the definition of family has become so much more fluid than 10 or 15 years ago. Your family is what you make of it and that's perfectly OK. I was perfectly happy and I didn't even have an inkling of curiosity, oh I guess I have a father. I wonder if I have siblings. That's something I've come to much later in life.

The most important thing I wish I'd known, it was a lot easier, thinking back, all the details of the back story. Obviously age appropriate, what your child will understand. It makes it a lot easier to explain to other people than to be caught off guard. From my perspective, I was quite happy, always knowing how I came to be, why I came to be, what determined that and I am happier for it.

During the question and answer period that followed her talk, Hannah got a question from the audience from the mother of two donor children who asked how she answers the question, "who is my dad?" The questioner wanted to know if it is okay to reply that she doesn't have a dad, she's a donor child.

Hannah replied:

> For people that were close to me, I would actu-
> ally explain, "well, it's my Mom, she wanted to
> have me." I added more detail as I got older. It's a
> lot easier now, people aren't going to think twice
> about it. OK, you used a donor or adopted. So
> it's a lot easier to be open and honest. Ultimately
> more beneficial to you because you are not go-
> ing to have to hide anything from your children,
> they're not going to see that anxiety in you and
> they will be more at peace with it. Okay, that's
> my family, that's fine. (7)

These three young people speak with compelling emotional
honesty about their experiences growing up with a single
parent by choice. They strongly urge you to be honest with
your child and, in an age appropriate way, let your child
know where he or she comes from - the back story of how
they came to be. They also emphasize the importance of being connected to other families like theirs even though their
family felt "normal" and the definition of family has become
so much more "fluid."

Choosing Not To Be a Single Parent

Jane Mattes, the founder of Single Mothers By Choice, offers this wisdom to those of you who decide not to pursue
becoming a parent on your own:

> If you decide not to, come up with another big
> plan so that it is not about this or nothing but it
> could be this or something having a child would

not have permitted. It is great to hear when people come to that conclusion that they really have a different dream [than having a child] especially these days when women are being pressured by their parents to do this which we never heard until the last few years. So, we have to say, is this your dream or theirs (8)

As Jane Mattes suggests, you are at risk of "accumulating regret" if you allow your dreams to go unfulfilled or you succumb to external pressures and fulfill others' dreams for you. However, if you follow Yalom's dictum not to accumulate regret and act decisively, this doesn't have to happen.

THE THIRD AGE

These days, as the average life span continues to lengthen, you and I can expect to live a very long time. The lengthening life span is a remarkable social phenomenon that has enormous impact. For example, Erik Erikson in "Identity and the Life Cycle" and Daniel Levinson in "The Seasons of a Man's Life and The Seasons of a Woman's Life " established the concept of human development over the life span, not just in childhood. However, only Peter Laslett, a British gerontologist, appears to have uniquely understood the social and psychological impact of our vastly increased longevity. According to his research on Britain and America, this remarkable demographic shift has been occurring since the 1980s. Considering human development over the life span in the context of our increasing longevity, he asks a crucial existential question: "How are we going to use this sudden, unprecedented, unanticipated release from mortality? (9) In his book, "A Fresh Map of Life: The Emergence of the of Third Age," (1991) he gives a very helpful answer.

In Laslett's conception of the increasing life span: "First comes an era of dependence, socialization, immaturity, and education, second an era of independence, maturity and responsibility, of earning and saving, THIRD, OF PERSONAL FULLFILLMENT [my emphasis] and fourth an era of decrepitude and death. (10). He notes that the Third Age "needs a fresh map of life, an intelligible guide to a [new] social landscape...a new world of experience [that] comes after our children have left us and after we have given up our jobs so as to enter what is now called the Third Age." (11).

Laslett's book was published in 1989, more than 20 years ago. Since then, while our life span keeps being extended so have our working lives. In contrast to the retirees at the time Laslett was writing, giving up our jobs - our means of economic survival - may not be possible in these tough economic times. Today, so many of us continue to work past the traditional "retirement" age, whether part-time or full-time, that the notion of retirement itself is being redefined. This new fluidity in the boundary between work life and retirement is referred to as "reinventing" or "redirecting" traditional retirement. In my personal experience with retirement, I came up with the term "working differently" to refer to this redefinition.

THE THIRD AGE, SOLO

Still another notable demographic shift Laslett did not take into account is that so many more of us are living solo as we reach the decade of our fifties and survive well into our eighties, nineties and for a growing number of us into our hundreds. When you enter or are in the decades of later life, what gives meaning and purpose to life on your own? How do you draw a map of the Third Age, your own "intelligible guide to a [new] social landscape" even if hours spent working or health concerns of these years limit the time you can devote to this new existential journey.

Two ways Laslett proposes to draw your map is to become a "trustee of the future" and a "cultural trustee."(12) By becoming a "trustee of the future" you use your capacities and expertise to provide guidance to those younger than you and help equip them with needed skills and knowledge. By becoming a cultural trustee, you guard and support the continued existence of vital cultural institutions. Laslett also suggests that you "direct your efforts to that which interests you in active cooperation with others with similar interests and outlooks."(13) I want to add another element to Laslett's guidelines - become a trustee of nature, that is, help preserve and protect the natural world.

Consider how these guidelines apply to you:

WHAT CAPACITIES AND EXPERTISE CAN YOU OFFER TO YOUNGER PEOPLE?

WHAT CULTURAL INSTITUTIONS AND PARTS OF THE
NATURAL WORLD CAN YOU GUARD AND SUPPORT?

WHAT INTERESTS DO YOU SHARE WITH LIKE-MIND-
ED PEOPLE THAT YOU CAN PURSUE IN COLLABORA-
TION WITH THEM?

You can draw a map to your Third Age by responding to
these questions. Moreover, by taking action on the basis of
your answers to these questions, you develop and express
what he calls a "Third Age attitude." (14)

Laslett not only saw the Third Age as a time of activity and
participation. He also recognizes that it can be a time of
withdrawal as in the more traditional retirement and the de-
clining activity of the Fourth Age. Being in the Third Age
gives you a choice. You decide your own balance between
withdrawal and participation.

Jane Enters the Third Age

Jane Mattes, the founder of Single Mothers by
Choice, entered her Third Age when her son
turned 24. "I needed to find something to think
about other than[my son]. I looked for something I loved. I had belonged to a plant society
before he was born so I rejoined because I love
plants. I am now on the Board and I have plants
all over my apartment."

Jane is also volunteering and interacting with the
staff at an agency that treats addiction as she has

a personal interest and expertise in this field of practice. She continues to work part-time in her own therapy practice as well as direct the organization she founded but she makes time for her love of plants, being involved in a horticultural society as well as her volunteer work. (15)

So, like many of us these days, Jane has not retired in the traditional sense but she has found a way to "work differently." That gives her time to be a "trustee of the future" in her volunteer work, to be a "trustee of nature" by being on the board of a horticultural organization and to pursue her interest in plants in collaboration with others.

GROW A NEW PART OF YOU

As a person on your own in the later decades of life, you may already feel sufficiently fulfilled by following the contours of the Third Age map you have drawn for yourself. Even so, there may still be another way to enrich life on your own. Consider developing a new part of yourself. In other words, grow some capacity, nurture some talent or pursue some ambition that has lain dormant or undiscovered. Perhaps you did not consider doing this before now because of family responsibilities or hours spent working full-time. That is how it happened for me.

I Find My Writing Voice

The time opened up to "grow a new part" of me when I gave up my full-time psychotherapy practice. I'd come up with the idea for "Living Solo" well over a year before coming to the decision to "work differently." I'd even written a detailed outline.

My work demands and my need and desire for "R and R" after working hours (rest and recreation) left my book idea unrealized. Also, I had never undertaken a project like this before, that is, writing a "self-help" book. I was not at all certain I was capable of doing so. Without devoting time to it, I would never know. The time did open up when I closed my full-time practice; Eventually, I got out my outline, I sat down at my desktop computer and began to write..

ON YOUR OWN BUT NOT ALONE

When you think about the years ahead:

DO YOU PLAN TO STAY IN THE HOME YOU ARE LIV-ING IN NOW?

DO YOU WONDER WHO WILL BE THERE TO CARE FOR YOU IN CASE OF ILLNESS OR LOSS OF MOBIL-ITY?

DO YOU HAVE ADULT CHILDREN LIVING NEARBY
YOU CAN COUNT ON AS YOU AGE?

DO YOU FEAR BECOMING SOCIALLY ISOLATED?

These are hard questions to face in the later decades of life
as we climb the age ladder solo. Indeed, an enduring and
frightening image of aging is that of a person who has become socially isolated and ends up living in an age-segre-
gated institutional setting where no one comes to visit. In
reality, especially in our seventies and older, social isolation
can result from losses such as the death of a spouse and
other family members or friends, or health problems inter-
fering with our mobility. Our families may then insist we
leave our communities and give up our homes to live in an
age segregated institutional setting. So, from an existential
perspective, your answers to these questions are crucial in
determining how you will live out your remaining years on
your own.

Choosing community-based living arrangements that pro-
mote social support and connection to others assures that
you can continue to live independently and still be on your
own but not alone. They assure you will be able to have
ongoing contact with a diverse group of people of all ages.
They also assure a much more affordable living arrangement
in contrast to continuing care retirement communities that
may require a large cash buy-in.

I have identified three different community-based living arrangements that provide social support, diversity and connection to others: These are: joining a "village," living in
cohousing and moving to be near adult children

Joining A Village

About 10 years ago, Susan, now age 75, got together with six of her neighbors [married and single] in Beacon Hill, Boston and founded Beacon Hill Village (16) Speaking about why, Susan put it this way: "All of us shared a sense our world will get smaller and we didn't want that. We didn't want to be the last living Beacon Hill person we knew." (17) What Susan and her neighbors wanted for themselves was to "age in place." They did not want to be sequestered in gated retirement communities, They also realized that, as the years pass, "spouses depart" so being able to stay within their community seemed especially important. In the popular press and research literature on aging, aging in place is defined as :"the preference of the majority of older adults to continue to live in a familiar environment...the ability to remain in one's residence of choice as one ages, avoiding unwanted relocation associated with age-related personal or environmental limitation. (18)

How did Susan and her neighbors get to age in place? They came up with the concept of a "village."

Founding Beacon Hill Village

We asked ourselves, what is there here? There is everything we need... in the way of doctors, entertainment, exercise, intellectual stimulation, generations. The city had it all. At some point, we realized we could be consolidators of services, call one number get the whole world, get anything you wanted, and there was going to be no rationing of services, no menus, buy in at this amount and you get to go to the doctor's once. We were people coming together to take care of ourselves... Fast forward [to today] our core members are single, older single women - our biggest success story." (19)

Currently, Susan notes that about 85 percent of the members of Beacon Hill Village are single. Judy Willet, the former Executive Director, explains that "it is more important for singles to be part of a community if you are aging alone. [People with partners] can care for each other." (20) Susan describes how Beacon Hill Village fosters a sense of connection among members:

We created a community so people could meet each other, we did the normal things: trips to the museum, apple picking in the summer. Certainly people began to meet each other, people who they didn't know before. We've come up with what we call affinity groups that don't require a staff running them, that are simply groups of people getting together with some common bond. (21)

The membership also varies considerably by age and includes people ranging in age from fifty to over one hundred with the average age being 76. Judy comments that "it is a strong, healthy independent group of people who choose to be part of Beacon Hill Village and a small part use it because they are frail and really need the services to stay in their own homes." (22)

Aging In Place In The Village

I asked Susan what happens when a member becomes ill or less physically active. She replied that the staff interfaces with the members, particularly when they begin to request more help. Then, the staff get to know them better and call them regularly. Beacon Hill Village also has many kinds of volunteers among its members so that someone will visit people who are shut-ins.

A Member of Beacon Hill Village Ages in Place

There was a woman who lived across the street from me who died at 102, staying in her own house. She ran a rooming house for 60 years and she had two sons, a bachelor who lived here and a son who was married and lived in California. All they wanted her to do was go to a nursing home so they wouldn't have to worry about her. Then they finally forced the issue and Dorothy said, "I won't go." She was then in her late eighties, early nineties. She said, "if I go to a nursing home, I won't be anybody but I am somebody here." And she was right. Eventually she needed somebody round the clock but she was still in her own home and people came to visit her. And on her 100th birthday they gave a party for her. (23)

Beacon Hill Village is now ten years old. Over the ten years of its existence, Beacon Hill Village became the prototype for other villages. An excerpt from its latest brochure nicely captures the essential components of a village:

> ~ a grassroots organization designed and governed
> by its members,
>
> ~ a staff concerned with the whole person and
> responsive to each members needs and wishes,
>
> ~ the host of diverse programs for mind and body,
>
> ~ a consolidator of an amazing variety of approved
> services and providers – often with discounts,
>
> ~ a connection to outstanding caregivers and
> medical practices,
>
> ~ a group enjoying the wisdom, generosity and
> talent of its volunteers, and
>
> ~ a non-profit entity supported by membership
> dues, donations and local foundations. (24)

Spearheaded by a vibrant national movement, there are now 90 open villages following the Beacon Hill Village model and 150 more in development around the country. There is also an umbrella organization, the Village to Village Network, founded to support the village movement. (25) Just a year ago, there were 60 open villages and 90 in development, a remarkable rate of growth. (26) Susan finds this "totally to our amazement. We were just trying to solve our own little problem (when) we started meeting in 1999. The winds of change had picked this up." (27)

Cohousing

Peggy became divorced in her mid-60's and, at first, she continued to live by herself in the house she and her spouse co-owned until it got sold in 1995. Then the reality of her finances and how she wanted to live hit her.

Peggy Chooses Cohousing

After the first year of separation, [I asked myself] where am I going to go? My initial thought was I love this place so much. The house is so nice, 13 acres surrounded by a salt marsh, it felt so good and so safe there. I thought, I can't move ever. Then I went to a workshop on finances. I heard this guy talk about finances and I went to see him. He asked me, 'how much are you willing to pay for a view?' I was going to have to come up with a whopping amount of money to buy his half of the house. So that knocked a little sense in me. So then I started looking around, where do I want to live. Then I was talking to a woman social worker I knew through PFLAG [Parents and Friends of Lesbians and Gays] and she told me, why don't you check out Midlife Options for Women. One of the things they had was a workshop for two Saturdays on shared housing. Oh, I'll go to that. It was very good and very interesting. The person who ran it lives in a big cooperative household with four owners and four members. They talked about everything from sharing an Apartment to COHOUSING [my emphasis]. Then I picked up some materials [about cohousing]. I liked the blend I can have my privacy and I can have my community. After recovering from hip surgery in 1994, I met some people in a North Shore Cohousing group, they had pot lucks and meetings. I got started there but that group went nowhere. Then I got connected to other co-housing people, I met people from Cambridge. They set up a meeting and I went to the first meeting. I felt this was going to go and it did happen. (28)

Originating in Denmark, cohousing was introduced into the United States more than 20 years ago. Cohousing communities share six common features:

~ Participatory process: Residents help organize and participate in the planning and design process and they are responsible as a group for final decisions

~ Deliberate neighborhood design: The physical design encourages a strong sense of community

~ Extensive common facilities: Common areas are an integral part of the community designed for daily use and to supplement living areas

~ Complete resident management: Residents manage the development, making decisions of common concern at community meetings

~ Non-hierarchical structure: Decision making is shared

~ Separate income sources: Residents have their own primary incomes. The community does not generate income. (29)

Peggy has lived in Cambridge Cohousing since it came into existence in 1998. Now, she tells me that "many of the 83 residents are retired. We were just turning into our sixties when we joined and now we are into our seventies. Eight members are octogenarians." (30) Peggy is one of the founding members who joined when she was in her sixties. Now that she is eighty years old, what about her aging in place?

Peggy Ages In Place in Cohousing

One of the places I looked at was an over 55 housing development. I thought, 'I don't want to live with this crowd.' They have more income than I have, a rich golf playing group. I did not want just to live with older people. Then I thought, 'I want a two bedroom apartment, a guest room, but I also may someday have someone living with me to take care of me.'

We are a caring community here but we are not a caretaking community. A group of us got together to talk about aging in community. We formed a new committee or task force. We first talked about how we envision aging and community, what do we envision our lives to be like, everybody there except one person said this is the place they'd be able to stay pretty much to the end of time." (31)

Having neighbors who check in with each other regularly and an emergency folder with the name of her primary care doctor and emergency contact located in the communal kitchen pantry supports Peggy's intention to stay at Cambridge Cohousing "to the end of [her] time." (32)

Moving Near Adult Children

Marilyn, age 77, decided to relocate to be near her adult children and grandchildren a few years after the death of her husband. Her son and daughter-in-law asked her to make the move for a number of reasons including to live more simply rather than carry the responsibility of the large house she shared with her spouse before his death, to live nearby so they could be there for her when health issues arose, and to be closer to her grandchildren. She took an apartment four blocks from her son and his family in a lively urban neighborhood that has a strong sense of community. Initially, however, although she knew she'd made the move so that she could age in place with the support of her adult children, she experienced an existential crisis. That is, Marilyn questioned the meaning and purpose of her life. In her words:

> I don't know what I expect from my life. I don't know how to spend my time. I don't know what gives me pleasure. Can I learn to live alone and not feel lonely. Why am I here? I have nothing to get up for. I am just pushing myself to get through the day. I miss my husband intensely. It's been two and half years, why do I still feel this way.

Marilyn expressed deep feelings of sadness and hopelessness as she asked these questions. I reflected back to her that she appeared to be in an existential crisis. She became curious about this. She then joined with me in exploring what the meaning and purpose of her life could be here in her new neighborhood and living near her adult children and grandchildren. Eventually, she had what she called a "Eureka" moment. In her words, "Wouldn't it have been wonderful if he could have moved here with me? [But] the past is gone. The dead are dead and I am here with family, my daughter-in- law, my grandchildren. They need me and I need them"

As this new awareness took hold, Marilyn got to be much closer emotionally to her grandchildren, son and daughter-in-law. She remembered how attentive and concerned her daughter-in-law had been on a day when Marilyn was feeling quite ill. She was thrilled when her daughter-in-law asked her to pick her grandchildren up at school one day. Two other grandchildren who lived farther away came to stay with her and she began to foster a closer relationship to them. She continues to cultivate connections to her neighbors as she had been doing all along but no longer needs to push herself to get up and out. By moving to age in place and becoming part of a family and a community, Marilyn has found meaning and purpose to her life.

Marilyn, Susan and Peggy have each found a different way to be on their own but not alone. However, there is something that they share. They live in their own homes in diverse neighborhoods where there is daily contact across the generations. Even if continuing care retirement communities were affordable to them, this would not be the living arrangement they would chose. They would miss intergenerational contact and diversity.

CHAPTER 3 ~ HEALTH & WELLBEING SOLO

Optimum physical health and emotional well being go hand and hand with being actively "out and about" and enjoyably nestling in at home. Of course, this is true for all of us, whether we live on our own or with another. However, taking very good care of yourself is especially crucial to living well solo because we need to depend so heavily on our own inner resources to do so. When we arrive home, no one is there to ask the proverbial "How was your day, dear?" Or, as a single 66 year old recently commented to me, "If I bump my elbow, no one is there asking me, are you OK?"

I have found that four areas of concern stand out in regard to maintaining health and well being on our own. The following questions capture these.

Ask yourself:

HOW MUCH DOES LONELINESS AFFECT YOUR WELL BEING?

IS YOUR LIVING SPACE A "COMFORT ZONE"?

DO YOU MISS TOUCH AND SEX?

SHOULD YOU BECOME SERIOUSLY ILL, DO YOU
WONDER WHO WILL CARE FOR YOU?

In the sections that follow, bringing in my own, my clients
and the experience of other single people with whom I have
spoken, I take up these questions. I also suggest how to
strengthen and expand the inner resources that will sustain
your health and wellbeing.

LONELINESS

A I began reflecting on loneliness, I became flooded with
song lyrics. Two lines of a particular song kept repeating in
my mind - the first and second lines of "Only the Lonely," a
song written and released by Roy Orbison in 1960.

> Only the lonely know the way I feel tonight,
> Only the lonely know this feelin' aint right

These simple lyrics powerfully convey an emotional truth:
loneliness is a unique and universal human feeling and it
causes us emotional distress. "Almost everyone feels the
pangs of loneliness at certain moments" as John Cacioppo
and William Patrick, two researchers on loneliness, observe.
They go on to say that loneliness can be, "brief and superfi-
cial" (1) but it can also be "acute and severe...and settle in
long enough to create a persistent, self reinforcing loop of
negative thoughts, sensations and behaviors." (2) Moreover,
if chronic, loneliness has serious consequences for our physical health.

Loneliness has been associated with alterna-
tions in the functioning of the cardiovascular,
endocrine and immune systems. A recent theo-
retical model of the correlates and consequences of loneliness posits that age-related declines
in physiological resilience are accelerated by
chronic loneliness…in younger adults, loneliness
has been associated with early markers of disease processes (e.g. subtle alterations in blood
pressure control mechanisms whereas in older
adults, loneliness is associated with frank disease
(e.g. elevated blood pressure) and dysregulation
across multiple physiological systems (e.g. impaired immune functioning and elevated levels of
stress hormones). (3)

I present my exploration of loneliness first in this chapter
because its impact on health is so significant and because
single people are at so much higher risk of feeling lonely. A
recent AARP study found that among people 45 years old or
older, the self reported rates of loneliness among single people were quite substantial - 45 percent for divorced people,
49 percent for separated people and 51 percent for people
who had never married compared to 29 percent for married
people. (4)

"Humans, after all, are inherently social beings." Cacioppo
and Patrick point out. They go on to say that "when people
are asked what pleasures contribute most to happiness, the
overwhelming majority [single or part of a couple] rate love,
intimacy and social affiliation above wealth or fame, even
above physical health." (5) But, what if we do not have the
love, intimacy and social affiliations we want? As the AARP

study shows, what if we experience an unfulfilled longing for connection with others, namely, loneliness.

Writers and researchers use different lenses from which to view and study loneliness. Two lenses I find especially useful are the social needs perspective and the social skills deficit perspective. As we delve deeper into how loneliness personally affects you, these two perspectives may give you a clearer sense of your own particular experience and how to respond to it.

The social needs perspective is based in attachment theory. Robert Weiss, in his landmark study, "Loneliness: The Experience of Emotional and Social Isolation" (1973) attributes emotional loneliness to the lack of a reliable attachment figure, e.g. not having a partner. Social isolation results from only having a few or no social affiliations such as in a religious congregation or in a community organization or in a social network like an extended family or stable group of friends. According to Weiss, lacking these relationships deprives us of nurturance and social integration, two essential features of attachment that counter lonely feelings.

The social skills deficit perspective links loneliness with certain affective, attitudinal and personality factors such as anxious and depressed mood, fear of being harshly judged by others, shyness, and low self esteem. These factors seem to associate much more with chronic loneliness rather than the more temporary loneliness that arises from certain life events such as the loss of a partner or a geographic move.

Let's consider the social needs perspective. Surely for many of us living solo, when we feel lonely, it is a partner we long for. But, finding a partner, a "reliable attachment figure" is uncertain - it may or may not happen.. If it does not happen, where will emotional nurturance come from – your fate mattering to someone else, having another person's interest and concern about your wellbeing? Like many single people, I have found the answer in friendship.

Of course, friendship is no substitute for a having a "significant other." Friendship offers a different kind of love, the affectionate regard termed "philia" by the Greeks' writing centuries ago, in contrast to "agape," the Greek word for the love between partners and family members. Reading this, are you taking the measure of your friendships with regard to mutual support and concern? Are you comfortable using a very important inner resource essential to getting that support and concern - a willingness to reach out to others, a willingness to let others know you are in need? In my clinical experience, if this willingness appears problematic for you, psychotherapy, both individual and group, can enable you to resolve this difficulty and begin to establish and sustain nurturing friendships. It does so by putting you in the position of leaning on someone else for emotional support maybe for the first time in your life.

The other dimension to the social needs perspective is social isolation vs. social integration. In the AARP survey, "lonely individuals tended to have an impoverished social network. They also reported fewer volunteering experiences and infrequent contact with family members and friends." (6) In contrast, the majority of non-lonely people volunteered time with non-profit organizations, charities, schools, hospital and religious organizations, showed high rates of participation in local community organizations and clubs and were in frequent contact with friends and family members in person, by telephone and online. (7) In this regard, do you take part in social groups? Are you part of a stable social network? As the AARP survey results show, reaching out and joining in counters the loneliness of social isolation.

The social deficit perspective brings up a crucial relationship between depressed mood and chronic loneliness, loneliness that lasts months and years. As Cacioppo, one of the researchers studying loneliness, found you are at much higher risk for depressed mood if you are chronically lonely and the reverse relationship may also be true. It is hard and perhaps unnecessary to determine cause and effect here. Rather, if you experience persistent feelings of sadness and hopelessness, low energy, a loss of interest in your usual activities as well as loneliness you may be a person who is both lonely and depressed. If so, it is imperative that you seek professional help. In my clinical experience, you may wish to consult your primary care physician as an effective and helpful first step.

Cacioppo notes that while loneliness is painful it has survival value. "Loneliness evolved like any other form of pain, it is what neuroscientists call an aversive state, meaning it signals us to change our behavior, in much the same way that hunger, thirst or physical pain do. So even though loneliness feels like it has no redeeming features, it motivates us to renew the connections we need to survive."(8)

Change the Mood

Inevitably, no matter how well connected we are, there may be many lonely moments as we go about life on our own. When this happened for Linda, a well socially connected woman in her mid - 60's, she found a strategy that she could make use of time and time again. Linda had been on her own for nine years after the death of her spouse. One Sunday afternoon in her Manhattan apartment, she felt terribly lonely. She could have stayed in this painful state but she chose to do something to ease her feeling. She took herself to the Central Park Carousel, bought ten tickets and rode around and around. As she rode, her lonely feeling was dissipated by the activity, the color and the music. Note that Linda called upon her inner resources and focused her attention on the here and now, away from an unfulfilled longing. Why not try to "Change the Mood" when next you find yourself in a lonely moment. Why not build a repertoire of mood-changing enjoyable activities you can reliably count on to dispel loneliness.

HOME AS A COMFORT ZONE

D.W. Winnicott, a noted British psychoanalyst who wrote a great deal about families and children once authored a book of essays entitled "Home Is Where You Start From." In it Winnicott stressed that when as children, we experience "home" in a psychological sense as a place of safety and security, we get the best start in life. I suspect that the experience of coming in your own door and the immediate feeling of comfort it brings is pretty much universal and is akin to the feeling of safety and security a child, if adequately cared for, experiences coming into the family home.

Unfortunately, not all of us have been given that "best start" because for a variety of reasons, our parents /caretakers, failed to provide a sense of safety and security. This can pose great difficulty for those of us who, as single adults, face making a "safe and secure" home for ourselves. Perhaps I should say, "safe and secure enough" because, of course, there is no perfectly safe and secure home in this hazardous world.

By making his home into a "comfort zone," Eric, a single man in his late thirties, demonstrates how empowering it can be to overcome a childhood legacy of feeling insecure and unsafe at home.

Eric

Eric came from a home that was disrupted by divorce when he was in elementary school. After the divorce, his parents lived in two different cities and eventually two different states. When Eric would visit his father each summer, he would find his possessions and his bedroom would have been appropriated by the children of the latest live-in partner of his father [of whom there were many]. This went on for a number of years.

When he became an adult, Eric spent very little time in the various apartments he occupied. In fact, he owned very little furniture and hung nothing on the walls. Through therapy, Eric became aware of his deep reluctance to make a home for himself and how it traced back to being displaced from his room in his father's house during the years he made summer visits. He then started to make a proper home for himself. This shift involved moving to a much nicer and larger apartment, buying furniture, and decorating according to his newly emerging tastes. He no longer avoids spending time at home and is enjoying his self created "safe and secure" nest.

As Dorothea found, the "home" feelings of safety and security are also vulnerable to loss later in life. Fortunately, as her experience tells us, she also found that they can be regained.

Dorothea

After Dorothea, a woman in her mid-forties, got divorced, the apartment which she owned jointly with her husband got sold. She and her young son then moved to a rented apartment where they lived for many years. Then her landlord informed her the property would soon be sold. Fortunately, she had received the proceeds from the sale of some property she owned with a sibling. She decided she would put it towards buying a place of her own.

This decision had a very positive impact on Dorothea's mood as she often would be tearful and sad at continuing to be on her own. Eventually, she found an apartment she wanted to buy, purchased it, did some renovations and moved in with her son. She felt completely ecstatic at doing this and told me she felt it was like "being in love." She's "in love" with her new apartment and with her new neighborhood where many people she knows live and frequently drop in.

Whatever its origin personally for you, whether early or later in life, you may now have become aware that your present home is not a "comfort zone" that is, you may not feel the degree of safety and security you would like to feel. As Dorothea and Eric show you, with an awareness of what we once had and lost in the past, we get another chance to make our homes into "comfort zones."

YOUR SELF CARE KIT

There are three areas of health and wellbeing that pose of particular challenge living solo. These are an absence of touch and sex in our everyday lives and a concern for how we will be cared for in the event of a serious health problem. The challenge they present is to tap into your inner and outer resources to find ways to take good care of yourself. I call this assembling your own "self care kit."

Sex

I have found considerable variation in a sense of sexual deprivation single adults feel. I also found that the intensity with which those of us living solo experience a sense of sexual deprivation seems to vary by age and stage in life. For example, a 32 year old states she feels chronically "sex starved" but in a generalized way, that is, without a specific person in mind. A 69 year old states she has been celibate since her divorce some years earlier but also states she does not miss sex. A 50 year old who longs to have a partner wonders if she is fated to wake up alone in bed for the rest of her life. The intensity and feeling of deprivation about sex seems to happen intermittently for most of us living solo - arriving, staying with us for a while but then leaving as our attention focuses elsewhere. In other words, you can count on your sense of deprivation about sex to abate but also to return at times perhaps depending on a certain trigger such as a memory, an image or even an internal hormonal shift.

Although the absence of regular sex with a partner is a fact of single life, does this mean that sexual satisfaction must also be absent? Betty Dodson who has been labeled the "Queen of Masturbation" obviously did not think so. As she proposed in her book, Sex for One: The Joy of Self Loving, "Masturbation is the ongoing love affair that each of us has with ourselves, throughout our lifetime."(10) Reading this may be bringing up some discomfort as masturbation is so infrequently spoken about and may carry a strict taboo for some of us. You may also be thinking that masturbation cannot substitute for sex with a partner. Of course, it can't. However, why not view it from Dodson's perspective as a form of self-loving and, if you have not already done so, add masturbation to your "self care kit". Her book provides a comprehensive "instruction manual" in how to do this for both men and women. As she developed her thinking and practice about self loving, she also began offering Bodysex Workshops in order to dispel inhibitions and teach optimum techniques just as a sex therapist might do working with a couple. These workshops still continue to be offered. (11)

Touch

Non-sexual touch through massage opened up a new and different world of physical experience to me. Over the years as a person on my own, massage was and still is the only reliable and safe way I can always count on being physically touched in intimate way by another adult. My first ever massage was a revelatory moment in life on my own. It happened that the massage therapist was a man so it was also the very first time I experienced touch by a man that was physically intimate but non-sexual. While experiencing the sensation of his hands on my body, I recall feeling soothed and cared for, a kind of physical comfort that I have found to be unique to the massage experience. No wonder for, as the neurobiologists have found, "a warm touch seems to set off the release of oxytocin, a hormone that helps create a sensation of trust, and to reduce levels of the stress hormone, cortisol."(9) I was not aware of this scientific finding at the time but I was aware of the comforting and pleasurable feelings it triggered. Ever since my first massage many years ago, massage has become a central element in my personal "self-care kit."

I often recommend massage to my clients, many of whom experienced "unsafe" touch and parental neglect as youngsters. Through therapy, they learn to become better caretakers of themselves, both emotionally and physically. Massage is one of the ways they learn to do this.

Missing physical touch may not be the situation you find yourself in. If you have a pet in life on your own, no doubt you are getting lots of touch albeit non-human. But, if you are missing intimate human touch, why not add massage to your self care kit.

Symbolic Chicken Soup

Being nurtured and cared for when we are ill is another of the special challenges single adults face. Speaking with a single friend who lives at a distance and who has had a number of health issues over the years, I came up with the phrase "symbolic chicken soup." On its own, "chicken soup" carries a practically universal connotation of maternal caring in our multi-ethnic culture. By adding the word "symbolic," I mean expressing caring without being physically present to convey concern or even that actual bowl of chicken soup. I did this countless times when my friend was ill. By sending my friend symbolic chicken soup, whether by phone, text or e-mail, I continue to nurture and care for her and she reciprocates when I have my own health issues.

Symbolic chicken soup can help us get through times of ill health when single life poses an increased risk of isolation and lack of emotional support. Although occasionally involving more serious health conditions such as post major surgery, I have mostly given and received symbolic chicken soup at times of relatively minor illness or health conditions. This form of self care may be familiar to you and your friends or, you may have to learn to reach out to people you know as Jack did (see Chapter 1).

Mutual nurturance at times of ill health usually takes place in an informal way. What if a more serious health issue arises for you, how will you be cared for? One answer may lie in creating a "support community" as Joan did.

Joan, A Cancer Patient

After being diagnosed with lung cancer. Joan gathered up of her friends in support of her care while she underwent chemotherapy. Her friends had been asking her what they could do to help. So, Joan set up a calendar where each of her friends could chose a day... when they were "on call" to run errands, fix a meal, take her on an outing or just visit. Joan created her community and her friends were grateful and felt useful (12)

NATURE AS A FAITHFUL COMPANION

You might well be asking why I now bring your attention to being in the natural world as a way to become more self nurturing. Perhaps you already have found the beauty of nature a source of solace in life on your own. I certainly have learned to. So has Jane Goodall, quoted here from in an interview in the Boston Globe about her new book "Seeds of Hope: Wisdom and Wonder from the World of Plants."

The peace of the forest has become part of my being. Indeed, if I close my eyes. I can transform the noise of loud talking or traffic in the street into the shouting of baboons or chimpanzees, the roaring of the wind through the branches or of the waves crashing onto the shore. (13)

What Jane Goodall and I have discovered is that being in

nature can provide a protective layer against an intrusive or disturbing external environment. It can even ease emotional pain. I describe exactly how this took place for me during a brief visit I made to Wellfleet, Cape Cod in the summer of 2012. As you may gather from my anecdote, the way in which nature can bring you into here-and-now is the emotional resource I referred to at the beginning of this section. I have found it to be a dependable way to relieve the emotional distress of loneliness at home or wherever I travel. Being in the immediacy of the moment allows us to be without a past or a future and, as I have gratefully found time and time again, dispense with any intermittent pain around being single.

Sonata For Unaccompanied Violin

I boldly booked two days in Wellfleet on Cape Cod because I so thoroughly enjoy being in nature there. Even knowing I would be there on my own, it turned out to be quite emotionally difficult. Wellfleet was full of many "duets" and "quartets," that is, couples and family groups but I only encountered one other "unaccompanied violin." So there I was, exploring the town and its environs, sitting out on the lawn where I was staying, eating meals all on my own. At moments, I felt painfully bereft of a companion but focusing on nature relieved the emotional distress I felt being on my own in such a family- and couple-oriented setting..

Binoculars in hand in search of bird life, I took long walks, observing the natural world around me as I walked in the nearby woods, alongside the salt marshes and the shoreline leading out of town. With my binoculars in front of my eyes and just walking along looking at the landscape, I was completely absorbed in the present moment, feeling a sense of emotional calmness. I was also being intellectually stimulated by being curious about what I was observing.

Nature continues to be my "faithful companion" and hopefully because it is readily available, can become yours,. Whether seeing the night sky as I stand by my apartment window, hearing the early morning twittering of bird or going on a day long nature outing, being in the here-and-now in nature, I can feel completely sufficient unto myself.

EPILOGUE ~ SOLO WITH HOPE

I can't go on, I'll go on.
  ~ Samuel Beckett

Over many years of clinical work with single adults and my own single life experience, I have found that, even as we may feel content much of the time, there can still be an underlying feeling of deprivation. This feeling understandably arises from the reality of lacking a partner. I have no doubt that many of us living solo experience a longing to have a partner at times. For me, this feeling comes into my awareness in especially poignant moments such as at weddings, seeing couples holding hands as I go out and about, planning a vacation, or perhaps most painful of all, family holidays.

You may have other "poignant moments" to add to this very personal list of mine. For example, after her divorce a woman in her mid-forties sadly recalled learning she'd been left out of a dinner party hosted by her married friends, a party that only included her other married friends. She also tearfully recalled feeling intensely alone and filled with longing for a partner while standing in her kitchen after hosting her own dinner party for married friends

I am not suggesting that "poignant moments" of longing to have a partner will never arise. On the contrary, of course they will. What concerns me as both a therapist and a person

on my own is the level of distress that being without a partner causes day to day. A useful clinical yardstick for assess-
ing the degree of emotional distress consists of three questions: how long a painful feeling persists, how intense it is,
and how much it affects how we function day-to-day. There
is a world of difference between a feeling of deprivation that
arises and then leaves in a fleeting sort of way versus one
that chronically stays with us. When you apply this yardstick
to how you personally experience the lack of a partner, what
degree of distress do you uncover? If a sense of deprivation
keeps intruding into your present moment, stays with you,
and continues to affect your mood, then you may well be in
too much emotional distress.

What troubles me even more about a chronic feeling of deprivation in relation to being without a partner is that hopelessness and a belief that this lack may never be remedied
often goes along with it. In actuality, many of us will remain circumstantially single but I distinguish this from being
emotionally single. By being circumstantially single, I mean
not only that life did not turn out as you expected and you
remain single but also that you do not dwell on this fact. Instead, you comfortably accept that it may not happen. When
you are emotionally single, a painful sense of despair about
being single is somehow always there with you. It frequently
breaks through into your everyday awareness. It can trigger
intense sadness and be accompanied by a pernicious belief
that you are not supposed to get what you want in life. Feeling and believing this way, you may want to consider speaking to a psychotherapist.

FROM EMOTIONALLY TO
CIRCUMSTANTIALLY SINGLE

The good news from my clinical and life experience is that there is a pathway from being emotionally single to being circumstantially single, that is, from emotional distress to emotional wellbeing living solo. Whereas the reality of being without a partner may not change, your feelings and beliefs can change. Then, you can look to the future with a sense of openness and shift your belief that you are doomed to lifelong singlehood, By reframing your being single in this way, you diminish its impact on your mood and your life in the present.

As I observed in Chapter 1, the process of change begins with self awareness. Through therapy or self reflection, consider whether you are emotionally single. As Chris Berdik, the author of "Mind Over Mind" insightfully asks: "How do unspoken expectations become self fulfilling prophecies?" (1) He notes: "The assumptions of self perception range beyond our corporeal selves (who we are and how we should act). The answers are awash in self fulfilling prophecies that can both enrich us and hold us back. By tweaking the expectations of self perception we can stretch the boundaries of who we are. (2)

Moreover, Berdik regards our "assumptions of self perception" as just as much about the ways we think about yourselves as about a "cognitive reflex" embedded in our neural networks. The findings of neurophysiology confirm that we can activate and modify our neural networks by new thoughts and feelings. You may recall from Chapter 1 how the extraordinary neuroplasticity of the brain allows us to map new neural pathways when we become aware of old attachment patterns, consciously think new thoughts and enact new behaviors.

What if you consciously shifted from believing you will never and are not meant to find a partner to believing that good things are supposed to happen to you? Try it out on your own. Or, even more effective in my experience: become aware of your underlying negative expectations by taking part in a therapy group and/or by seeing a therapist. With supportive feedback from other group members or a therapist, you can learn to think positively about your possibilities. Then, if one of those good things that you want does not happen such as meeting a partner, it will not be because it was not meant to happen for you but because external circumstances were such that it did not happen.

As always a change in behavior is an important corollary to a shift in beliefs. When asked how we can shift from feeling in a dead end to viewing life with a sense of possibility, a very wise clinician answered this way: "GO OUT AND LIVE A RICH LIFE." (3) When I was in my twenties, I found myself raising two children on my own. I told a therapist I was seeing at the time how empty my life as a single adult woman felt. I remember being asked, "Well, what is it you want to do?" Back then, I didn't know how to enrich my life as a woman on my own. I do now. That is what I want for all of you who are living solo. Through self awareness, to know yourselves and to find ways to enrich your lives so each day is meaningful, purposeful, self-nurturing, enjoyable, socially connected and, with a well-stocked self care kit, adds to your physical and emotional wellbeing.

Boston, 2013

NOTES

Introduction

1. Carlo Rotella, "The New Normal: Living Alone." The Boston Globe, November 10, 2010.
2. Erik Klinenberg, "One's A Crowd," The New York Times, February 5, 2012.

Chapter 1

1. Many articles and books discuss the theory and research findings of the attachment theorists, John Bowlby and Mary Ainsworth. For a comprehensive review and bibliography, see the Wikipedia entries for Attachment Theory and Affectional Bonds.
2. Latchkey Kid. A child who arrives home after school, lets himself/herself into the house—with a latchkey and is unattended until the parent(s) arrive(s) home from work. The Free Dictionary.com.
3. S. Hofferth, A Bayfield, S. Deich and P. Holcomb, The Future of Children. National Child Care Survey. The Urban Institute. 1991.
4. Tanya Scheffer and P. Naus. "The Relationship Between Fatherly Affirmation and a Woman's Self Esteem, Fear of Intimacy, Comfort with Womanhood and Comfort with Sexuality," Canadian Journal of Human Sexuality. (1999)/ 8:1.
5. Peggy Streep, "Sons of Unloving Mothers: The Same Wounds and Then Some. It's not just the daughter who is hurt. www.PsychologyToday.com/blog/tech-support/201305/son-unloving-mothers-the-same-wounds-and-then-some.
6. Ibid.

7. Ibid.

8. Rachel Rettner. "Overparenting Leads to Undesirable Traits Study Shows." MSNBC.com June 6, 2011. See also T. Lemoyne and T. Buchanan. "Does 'Hovering' Matter?   Helicopter Parenting and Its Effect on Wellbeing," July/August 2011. Sociological Spectrum.

9. Mary Ainsworth. Five Criteria in "Attachments Beyond Infancy," American Psychologist. 1989. Volume 44.

10. Erin York Cornwell and Linda J. Waites. "Perceived Isolation and Health Among Older Adults," Journal of Health and Social Behavior. 2009. 50:1.

Chapter 2

1. Personal Communication, January 13, 2012.

2. Ibid.

3. Ibid.

4. Ibid.

5. Personal Communication, February 17, 2012.

6. Personal Communication, March 17, 2013.

7. DVD Recording, Panel Discussion with Three Adult Children of Single Mothers By Choice, October 15, 2011.

8. Personal Communication, January 13, 2012.

9. Peter Laslett, A Fresh Map of Life: The Emergence of the Third Age. Harvard University Press. 1991.

10. Ibid. p.4.

11. Ibid. p. vii.

12. Ibid. p. 157.

13. Ibid.

14. Ibid.

15. Personal Communication, February 24, 2012.

16. Personal Communication, February 29, 2012.

17. Ibid.

18. Andrew Scharlach, Carrie Graham and Amanda Leh-

ing. "The Village Model: A Consumer Driven Approach For Aging in Place," The Gerontologist Advance Access. August 25, 2011.

19. Personal Communication, February 29, 2012.
20. Personal Communication, February 7, 2012.
21. Personal Communication, February 29, 2012.
22. Personal Communication, February 7, 2012.
23. Personal Communication, February 29, 2012.
24. "Connect, Discover and Enjoy." Beacon Hill Village Brochure.
25. www.vtvnetwork.org
26. Ibid.
27. Personal Communication, February 29, 2012.
28. Personal Communication, December 29, 2011.
29. Charles Durrett. The Senior Co-Housing Handbook. New Society Publishers. 2009.
30. Personal Communication, December 29, 2011.
31. Ibid.
32. Ibid.

Chapter 3
1. John Cacioppo and William Patrick. Loneliness: Human Nature and the Need for Social Connection. W.W. Norton. 2008. p. 7.
2. Ibid. p. 7.
3. John Cacioppo. University of Chicago, Department of Psychology. www.Psychology.Uchicago.edu/people/faculty/Cacioppo/jtcreprints/hc09.pdf
4. C. Wilson and B. Moulton. Loneliness Among Older Adults 45 Plus. Prepared by Knowledge Networks and Insight Policy research. AARP. Washington, D.C. 2010.
5. Cacioppo and Patrick, p. 7.
6. C. Wilson and B. Moulton, p. 17.
7. Ibid.

8. John Cacioppo, quoted in E. Dwyer, "Understanding Loneliness: How Older Adults Can Stave Off The Effects of Chronic Loneliness." AARP Magazine. September 24, 2010.

9. Benedict Carey. "Evidence That Little Touches Do Mean So Much," The New York Times, February 23, 2010.

10. Betty Dodson. Sex for One: The Joy of Self Loving. Crown Trade Paperbacks. 1987.

11. See the website www.babeland.com for listings of workshops in their various retail store locations.

12. Judy Costlow, "Keeping the Gold in the 'Golden Years' – Staying Healthy As We Age." The Women's Health Activist . March-April 2013, p. 3.

13. The Boston Globe, March 18, 2013.

Epilogue

1. Chris Berdik. Mind Over Mind The Surprising Power of Expectations. Current Division of Penguin Press. 2012. p. 143.

2. Ibid. p. 126.

3. Personal Communication, Dr. Phyllis Cohen.

REFERENCES

DePaulo, Bella. Singled Out: How Singles Are Stereotyped, Stigmatized and Ignored and Still Live Happily Ever. 2006. St. Martins Press.

Erikson, Erik. Identity and the Life Cycle. 1980. WW Norton Co.

Falk, Florence. On My Own: The Art of Being A Woman Alone. 2007. Harmony.

Fischler, Marcelle. "A Home Without Prince Charming." 2009. The New York Times. December 12.

Gross, Jane. "Aging At Home: For the Lucky Few. 2006. The New York Times. February 9.

Huebeck,Elizabeth." Age Raises Fertility Risk for Men, Too." www.medicine.net

Klinenberg, Erik. Going Solo: The Extraordinary Rise and Surprising Appeal of Living Alone. 2012. The Penguin Press.

Krull, Erika. "Divorce – What Girls Miss When Dad Leaves Home." www.psychcentral.com

Koch, Wendy. "Number of Single Men Adopting Foster Kids Doubles." 2007. USA Today. June 14,

Llamas, Dr. Daniela. "Pausing the Biological Clock." 2013. The Boston Globe. Sept. 30.

Levinson, Daniel. The Seasons of a Man's Life. 1978. Ballantine Books.

Levinson, Daniel. The Seasons of a Woman's Life. 1996. Alfred Knopf.

Minuchin, S. Montalvo, B. Guerney, B., Rosman, B. and

Shumer, F. Families of the Slums. 1967. Basic Books.
Montagu, Ashley. Touching: The Human Significance of Skin. 1971. Harper and Row.

Navaroo, Mireya. "The Bachelor Life Includes a Family." 2008. The New York Times. September 7.

Parentification and Parentified Children. www.outofthefog. net.

Reinventing Aging. Harvard School of Public Health 2004.. Met Life Foundation Initiative on Retirement and Civic Engagement.

Schneider, E. Lynn. "Attachment Theory and Research: A Review of the Literature." 1991. Clinical Work Journal. 19:3.

Spira, Lucille and Richards, Arlene. "On Being Lonely, Socially isolated and Single: A Multi-Perspective Approach." 2003. Paper Available on-line.

Weiss, Robert, ed. Loneliness: The Experience of Emotional and Social Isolation. 1973. The MIT Press.

Winnicott, D.W. Home is Where You Start From. 1990. Penguin Books.

Winnicott, D.W. "The Capacity to be Alone" in The Maturational Process and the Facilitating Environment. 1996. International Universities Press.

Yalom, Iriving. Staring at the Sun: Overcoming the Dread of Death. (2008). Piatkus.